Idaho

by Fran Hodgkins

Consultant:
Dr. Dan Prinzing
Social Studies Coordinator
Idaho Department of Education

Capstone
press®
Mankato, Minnesota

Capstone Press
151 Good Counsel Drive • P.O. Box 669 • Mankato, Minnesota 56002
http://www.capstone-press.com

Library of Congress Cataloging-in-Publication Data
Hodgkins, Fran, 1964–
      Idaho / by Fran Hodgkins.
      v. cm.—(Land of liberty)
      Includes bibliographical references (p. 61) and index.
      Contents: About Idaho—Land, climate, and wildlife—The History of Idaho—
Government and politics—Idaho's economy and resources—People and culture.
      ISBN-13: 978-0-7368-1580-2 (hardcover)
      ISBN-10: 0-7368-1580-5 (hardcover)
      1. Idaho—Juvenile literature. [1. Idaho.] I. Title. II. Series.
F746.3 .H63 2003
979.6—dc21   2002012073

Summary: An introduction to the geography, history, government, politics, economy,
resources, people, and culture of Idaho, including maps, charts, and a recipe.

Editorial Credits
Tom Adamson, editor; Jennifer Schonborn, series and book designer;
      Angi Gahler, illustrator; Deirdre Barton, photo researcher; Eric Kudalis,
      product planning editor

Photo Credits
Cover images: Snake River, Unicorn Stock Photos/Patti McConville;
      Sawtooth Range, Idaho Travel Counsel

Bruce Coleman Inc./Kike Calvo, 50; Capstone Press/Gary Sundermeyer, 27 (left),
54; Corbis/ChromoSohm Inc./Joseph Sohm, 34; Corbis/Karl Weatherly, 4;
Corbis/Mark Gibson, 40; Courtesy Frederic Remington Art Museum, Ogdensburg,
New York, 24, 58; Gnass Photo Images/Jon Gnass, 8, 15, 18–19; Idaho State
Historical Society, 30–31; Idaho Travel Counsel, 44–45; Idaho Travel Counsel/Sun
Valley Company, 43; Index Stock Imagery/Carmen Northen, 48; Index Stock
Imagery/Mark Gibson, 16; Index Stock Imagery/Tim Brown, 22; Michael Haynes,
27 (right); Montana Historical Society, 29; One Mile Up, Inc., 55 (both); Photo
courtesy Larry EchoHawk and the Idaho Attorney General's Office, 38; PhotoDisc,
Inc., 1, 10, 56, 63; Robert McCaw, 57; Unicorn Stock Photos/Paula Harrington,
21; Unicorn Stock Photos/Travis Evans, 12–13; U.S. Bureau of Reclamation,
Pacific Northwest Region, 32; U.S. Postal Service, 59

Artistic Effects
Corbis, Corel, Digital Vision, and PhotoDisc, Inc.

1 2 3 4 5 6   08 07 06 05 04 03

Table of Contents

White-water rafters enjoy the challenge of Idaho's fast-moving rivers.

Chapter 1

About Idaho

The huge wave forces the nose of the raft upward until it seems to be pointing straight up at the sun. The rafters feel as though their rubber raft might go over backwards. Suddenly, the raft slams back onto the river with a teeth-rattling jolt. The rafters tighten their grips on their paddles before plunging them back into the water. All around the raft, the Snake River's rapids roar and foam. The foam makes the fast-moving water appear white.

Every year, thousands of people go white-water rafting on Idaho's rivers. They enjoy the adventure while seeing some of the most amazing mountain scenery in the country.

Did you know...?
Idaho has 82,747 miles (133,165 kilometers) of rivers. If all of Idaho's rivers were laid end to end, they would wrap around the world more than three times.

The Gem State

Idaho is one of the states that include the Rocky Mountains. The name Idaho was once thought to mean "Gem of the Mountains" in an American Indian language. But the word Idaho did not really exist. This name was made up because it sounded like an American Indian word. Names of states that came from Indian words were popular in the mid-1800s.

In 1863, the U.S. Congress named the territory Idaho thinking the name meant "Gem of the Mountains." The nickname Gem State stuck. Idaho does contain many gems, including the state gem, the star garnet.

People usually collect gemstones for their beauty. The word gem is also used to describe anything that is beautiful. Idaho's nickname reflects its beautiful scenery. Idaho has many wild rivers and towering mountains. The state's rivers feature more than 3,000 miles (4,800 kilometers) of white water.

Idaho is part of the northwestern United States. Montana and Wyoming border Idaho to the east. Washington and Oregon make up the western border. South of Idaho are Nevada and Utah. Canada lies to the north.

Idaho Cities

CANADA

WASHINGTON

Kootenai

• Coeur d'Alene

Coeur d'Alene

Lewiston •

Nez Perce

OREGON

MONTANA

IDAHO

Legend

American Indian Reservation

⭐ Capital

● City

〜 River

Scale
Miles
0   30   60   90
0   30   60   90   120
Kilometers

⭐ Boise

Sun Valley •

Arco •

Idaho Falls •

Shoshone-Bannock

Snake River

Twin Falls •

• Pocatello

Shoshone-Paiute

WYOMING

NEVADA   UTAH

The Sawtooth Range in central Idaho is the best known of Idaho's many mountain ranges.

Chapter 2

Land, Climate, and Wildlife

Idaho was the last of the 48 connected states to be visited by white explorers. Since then, people have been drawn to Idaho's mountain scenery.

Mountains make up most of the northern part of Idaho. Idaho's mountain ranges include the Sawtooth Range, the Salmon River Mountains, and the Bitterroot Range, which forms the Idaho-Montana border.

Idaho's many mountains make it a high-altitude state. Its average altitude is 5,000 feet (1,524 meters) above sea level. The state's lowest point is 770 feet (235 meters) above sea level where the Snake River flows through Lewiston.

The southern part of Idaho flattens out into the Snake River Plain. Farmers raise potatoes, sugar beets, and wheat on this broad, flat grassland.

Forests

Forests cover about 40 percent of the state. Idaho has several national and state forests. Many of the trees are western white pine, Idaho's state tree. Other evergreens found there are hemlock, Engelmann spruce, Douglas fir, and lodgepole pine. The forests also include maple, aspen, willow, and birch trees.

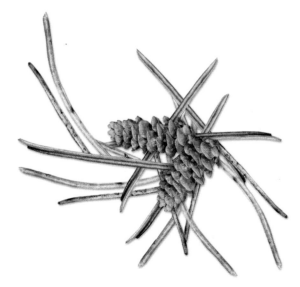

Idaho's Land Features

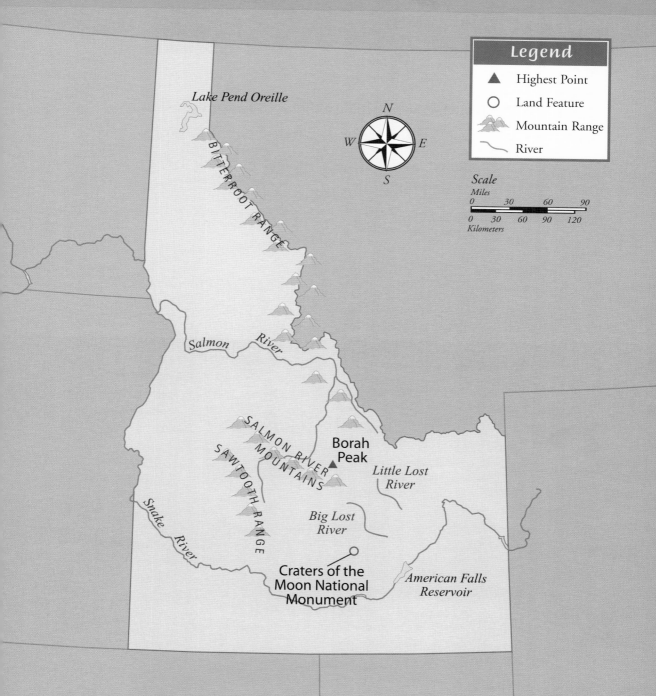

Lake Pend Oreille

BITTERROOT RANGE

Salmon   River

Legend

▲ Highest Point
○ Land Feature
⛰ Mountain Range
〰 River

Scale
Miles
0   30   60   90
0   30   60   90   120
Kilometers

SALMON RIVER MOUNTAINS

SAWTOOTH RANGE

Borah Peak

Little Lost River

Big Lost River

Snake River

Craters of the Moon National Monument

American Falls Reservoir

11

Rivers and Lakes

Most of Idaho's rivers have several miles of white-water rapids. The state also has more than 2,000 lakes.

In the central part of Idaho, two rivers disappear. The Big Lost River and the Little Lost River both flow into a field of hardened lava. They run underground for 120 miles (193 kilometers).

The Salmon River is also called the "River of No Return." The Salmon got its nickname because it has a very strong current. White-water rapids challenge skilled kayakers and rafters. Not until motorized boats were invented could people ride upstream on this 420-mile (676-kilometer) river.

The Snake River is another long river in Idaho. It runs through the Snake River Plain from Montana in the east to

The Salmon River is one of the main branches of the Snake River. It begins in the Sawtooth Range. It winds north then west to the Snake River.

"... the river ... is almost one continuous rapid ... the passage with canoes is impossible."

—William Clark, one of the first explorers to see Idaho

Washington in the west. It is 1,038 miles (1,670 kilometers) long. The Shoshone people called the Snake River the "River of the Sagebrush Plain." Along its route, the Snake River brings water to some of the state's driest areas. It provides water for farms and cities. Fourteen dams on the Snake River produce hydroelectric power. Power plants at the dams can use the flowing water to make electricity.

Shoshone Falls is the largest waterfall on the Snake River. Located near the city of Twin Falls, Shoshone Falls is higher than Niagara Falls. The water plunges 212 feet (65 meters) over the steep rock ledges. The Shoshone caught salmon at the bottom of the falls. The falls are too steep for the fish to swim upstream beyond this point.

Lake Pend Oreille (PON dor-AY) is the largest of Idaho's lakes. It covers 180 square miles (466 square kilometers). Lake Pend Oreille is also very deep. Its deepest point is

Shoshone Falls is the largest waterfall on the Snake River. The Shoshone called the waterfall "hurling waters leaping."

Lake Pend Oreille, located near Sandpoint, is Idaho's largest lake.

Did you know...?
Of the rivers in the connected 48 states, Idaho's Salmon River is the longest river that flows entirely within a single state.

1,158 feet (353 meters). That makes it the fifth deepest lake in the country.

Some of Idaho's lakes are artificial. People build dams across rivers to block the flow of the water. The water pools behind the dam and forms a lake. In Idaho, the largest artificial lake is American Falls Reservoir.

Climate

Just as Idaho's land varies, so does its climate. On the Snake River Plain, yearly precipitation averages between 8 and 20 inches (20 and 51 centimeters). The northern mountain areas get about 50 inches (127 centimeters) of precipitation each year.

The Pacific Ocean is the source of most of this moisture. During winter, a great deal of snow piles up in Idaho's mountains. Sun Valley gets 220 inches (559 centimeters) of snow per year. Melting snow can cause floods, especially during April and May.

Temperatures in Idaho vary with altitude and location. Higher altitudes in the mountains are usually colder. The southern part of the state and lower altitudes are usually warmer. Long periods of either very hot or cold weather are rare.

Wildlife

Idaho is home to many types of birds and animals. Beavers, minks, frogs, lizards, snakes, turtles, and other small animals live throughout the state. Elk, moose, deer, mountain lions, and bear live in the forests and plains.

Mountain areas are home to the bighorn sheep and the mountain goat. Lewis and Clark led the first expedition into what is now Idaho. Before they saw mountain goats in their travels in Idaho, white people did not know the fuzzy white goats existed.

Many of the animals and plants in Idaho are threatened or endangered. The grizzly bear is the largest threatened species. These bears can weigh up to 600 pounds (272 kilograms). Federal and state wildlife officials are trying to preserve the

Great amounts of snow can pile up in Idaho's mountains.

Woodland Caribou

Idaho is home to the most endangered large mammal in the lower 48 states. Only about 35 woodland caribou live in one small herd. This herd moves between northern Idaho, northeastern Washington, and southern British Columbia, Canada. Woodland caribou live in forested areas in small groups. They have large feet for walking through snow.

To restore the American herd, scientists bring woodland caribou into Idaho from Canada. The caribou are held in pens for several days and then released into the woods. Scientists watch both the new caribou and the native ones to see what they eat, where they go, and how they survive.

state's grizzlies and bring in new ones. But it takes a long time for the grizzly population to grow. A female grizzly has cubs only once every three years. Another problem for the grizzlies is the lack of room to roam. A male grizzly needs a territory of up to 400 square miles (1,000 square kilometers).

By the 1930s, hunting nearly wiped out the grizzly and the gray wolf. These animals are now coming back slowly, but people have mixed feelings about these predators. Most people want to protect wildlife. They also like to hike or camp in the woods. They develop land away from cities. These activities make an encounter with one of these dangerous animals likely.

Woodland caribou have broad antlers. This mammal is an endangered species.

21

Ancient native peoples painted or carved pictures into rock.

Chapter 3

History of Idaho

People have lived in Idaho for thousands of years. Archaeologists have found old tools, hunting weapons, pottery, and artwork left by these people. The artwork was painted on the walls of caves or carved into rock. The carvings can be seen today at several places, including Hells Canyon Recreation Area.

Descendants of those first people formed several American Indian tribes. They include the Coeur d'Alene, the Bannock, the Kootenai, and the Pend d'Oreille. The two largest groups were the Nez Perce and Shoshone. The Nez Perce were famous for breeding the strong, swift, spotted horse called the Appaloosa. The Shoshone were also known for their skill with

horses. American explorers depended on the horses of
the Nez Perce and Shoshone.

Lewis and Clark

Of the lower 48 states, Idaho was the last to be visited by white
explorers. In 1803, President Thomas Jefferson bought the

Lewis and Clark
(seated) were guided
on their expedition
by Sacagawea.

Louisiana Territory from France. The deal to buy the land was called the Louisiana Purchase. The territory more than doubled the size of the United States. Americans did not know what was in this new land. Only a few French fur trappers knew much about this area.

Jefferson sent Meriwether Lewis and William Clark to explore the area. He hoped they would discover a river that linked the Mississippi River with the Pacific Ocean. He also hoped they would find living mastodons and giant ground sloths. These creatures had been discovered only as fossils.

On May 14, 1804, Lewis and Clark set out from Illinois with a group of explorers. Over many months, they made their way north and west. They explored Idaho and eventually reached the Pacific Ocean. They did not find a river connecting the Mississippi River and the Pacific Ocean. They did not find mastodons and giant ground sloths, either. They did find many natural wonders and amazing creatures that had been unknown to white people. They discovered the pronghorn, which can run as fast as 60 miles (97 kilometers) per hour, and the shaggy white mountain goat.

In 1806, Lewis and Clark returned to Washington, D.C., with their reports. Their news made people interested in settling in Idaho. Traders arrived to trap animals for their fur. They set up trading posts. Soldiers built forts. Christian missionaries then established schools and churches. The Jesuits, a group of Catholic priests, founded the Coeur d'Alene Mission of the Sacred Heart near Desmet in 1842. It still exists today.

More Settlers

Gold was discovered in California in 1849. Thousands of people traveled through Idaho on their way to the gold fields. The route they took is known as the Oregon Trail.

In 1860, Elias Pierce found gold in Orofino Creek, Idaho. Many people moved to Lewiston and Idaho City. By 1863, Idaho City was the Northwest's largest city with a population of more than 6,000. That year, Congress named Idaho a territory.

More white settlers arrived in Idaho over the next several years. American Indians were pushed farther from their lands. The Coeur d'Alene, Bannock, Nez Perce, and Shoshone all fought back. They were defeated by the U.S. military.

Sacagawea

Lewis and Clark would not have been as successful as they were without the help of one Corps of Discovery member. As a child, a young Lemhi-Shoshone woman named Sacagawea was kidnapped from her people and taken to live with the Mandan tribe. While there, she married a French trapper. When the trapper joined Lewis and Clark as an interpreter, Sacagawea joined too.

Sacagawea stayed with Lewis and Clark for the entire journey. She helped Lewis and Clark talk with native people. She also helped them follow their route. Her presence let other American Indians know that the group was not a war party. She carried her baby son with her on the journey, another sign that the group was peaceful.

To honor her memory, the United States introduced the Sacagawea dollar in 2000. One side of the coin shows her and her baby.

"I am tired of fighting . . . The little children are freezing to death . . . My heart is sick and sad. From where the sun now stands, I will fight no more forever."

—*Chief Joseph, Nez Perce leader*

In 1877, the Nez Perce nearly won their fight. They defeated the U.S. Army at White Bird Canyon in northern Idaho. But more soldiers arrived and forced the Nez Perce to retreat. They tried to escape to Canada. Chief Joseph led the retreat. Many Nez Perce died along the way. Chief Joseph did what he thought was best for his people and surrendered to the Army just 42 miles (68 kilometers) from the Canadian border.

Statehood

Gold and silver drew new settlers to Idaho. The area grew quickly from 1860 to 1890. With the increase in population, Idaho could become a state. Idaho became a state on July 3, 1890.

During the 1900s, Idaho juggled the need to grow with the need to save its natural resources. Farmers and ranchers used the land for crops and cattle. Miners dug for silver, lead, gold, and other minerals. Lumber workers cut down thousands of trees, and fur trappers killed thousands of beavers.

In the late 1890s, troubles between mine owners and miners became violent. The miners formed a union to try to get better treatment and wages. The mine owners fired them. The miners fought back by blowing up mines. In 1905, the violence led to the murder of former governor Frank Steunenberg. He had called in federal troops to calm the violence. One union member, Frank Orchard, confessed to Steunenberg's murder.

Chief Joseph was a Nez Perce leader. He is famous for leading his people on a retreat through Idaho.

The 1900s

When the Great Depression (1929–1939) hit, many Idahoans suffered. The federal government set up programs to help people find work. One of them, the Rural Electrification Administration, brought electricity to farms.

The Great Depression ended with World War II (1939–1945). About 65,000 Idahoans served in the war. Many others grew food and supplied materials for the war effort.

During World War II, Idaho was the site of an internment camp. The U.S. government feared that people of Japanese

descent would help the enemy. Many Japanese Americans were sent to camps. Nearly 13,000 Japanese men, women, and children were kept in the internment camp near Twin Falls, Idaho.

In 1949, a science lab in southeastern Idaho began experimenting with nuclear energy. The National Reactor Testing Station made the world's first usable nuclear energy in 1951. Four light bulbs were lit using nuclear power. The experiment showed that nuclear energy could be used for electricity in homes.

Thousands of Japanese Americans were sent to an internment camp in Idaho during World War II.

In 1976, the Teton Dam burst and flooded several towns.

The Late 1900s

Throughout the late 1900s, Idahoans disagreed about land use. Some people wanted to use the land and its resources. Others wanted to preserve them for the future.

Mining has provided work for thousands of people. But mining can be destructive. Chemicals must be used to separate minerals from rock. These chemicals cause pollution.

Some open-pit mines strip away all of the earth covering a mineral deposit. Open-pit mining leaves huge scars on the land.

Dams built on Idaho's rivers have helped provide electricity to the state's citizens. But dams change the nature of rivers and the environment. Sometimes, disaster can strike. In 1976, the Teton Dam gave way, flooding towns with more than 75 billion gallons (284 billion liters) of water. The disaster killed 11 people and caused $500 million in damage.

Dams have also hurt the salmon population. Salmon live in the ocean most of their lives. When they lay their eggs, they return to the freshwater rivers where they were born. The dams have stopped many salmon from returning to their rivers. State officials and experts are working together to find ways to bring the salmon back.

Idaho's capitol is heated by geothermal energy. Water from a nearby hot spring is pumped to the building for heating.

Chapter 4

Government and Politics

Idaho has a history of advanced ideas in politics. In 1896, Idaho women were allowed to vote in state elections. This was more than 20 years before the U.S. government gave women the right to vote. In 1914, Idaho voters elected Moses Alexander to serve as governor. He was the first Jewish governor in American history. In 1990, Larry EchoHawk was elected state attorney general. He was the first American Indian elected to serve as a state's top legal official.

The state capital is Boise, which is also Idaho's largest city. State senators and representatives meet in the capitol building. The capitol's design is similar to that of the U.S. Capitol in

Washington, D.C. A solid copper eagle sits on top of the dome. The eagle is more than 5 feet (1.5 meters) tall and weighs 250 pounds (113 kilograms).

State Government

Like the U.S. government, Idaho's state government has three branches. The governor is the head of the executive branch. The governor sends bills to the legislature and signs bills into law. The lieutenant governor takes over if the governor is unable to serve out his or her term. Most of the state's governors have been Republicans.

Idaho has 35 legislative districts. Each district has one senator and two representatives who serve two-year terms. Voters in each district elect these three people to represent them in state government. Legislative sessions begin in January and usually last 90 days.

In 2002, Idaho had the nation's biggest legislative majority. Of the 35 members of the state senate, 32 were Republicans,

Idaho's State Government

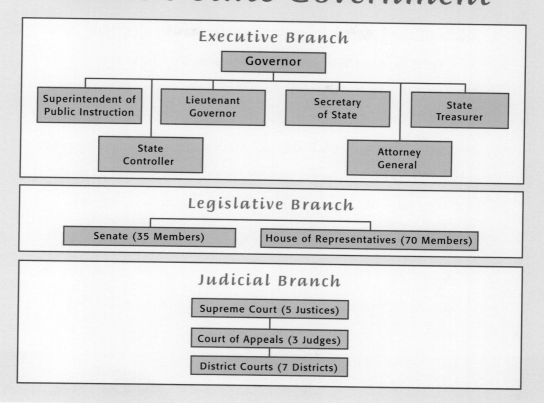

Executive Branch

Governor

Superintendent of Public Instruction | Lieutenant Governor | Secretary of State | State Treasurer

State Controller | Attorney General

Legislative Branch

Senate (35 Members) | House of Representatives (70 Members)

Judicial Branch

Supreme Court (5 Justices)

Court of Appeals (3 Judges)

District Courts (7 Districts)

and only three were Democrats. Sixty-one of the house of representatives' 70 members were Republicans. The rest were Democrats. Such a large number of lawmakers belonging to one political party is called a "supermajority."

Because of this supermajority, members of the Democratic Party have a hard time making themselves heard on issues.

Most of the lawmakers may have already decided how they will vote before the legislature meets as a group.

Like all other states, Idaho elects two senators to serve in the U.S. Senate. Idaho is also divided into two Congressional districts. Voters in each district elect a representative to serve in the U.S. House of Representatives. One district is in the western part of the state. The second district covers the eastern part.

Larry EchoHawk was the first American Indian to serve as a state's attorney general.

Larry EchoHawk

Larry EchoHawk, a member of the Pawnee tribe, was born in Orem, Utah. In 1973, he earned a law degree from the University of Utah. In 1977, he was named chief general counsel to the Shoshone-Bannock tribes at Fort Hall Reservation in Idaho. In 1982, he was elected to the Idaho house of representatives as a Democrat.

In 1990, he was elected attorney general, the state's highest law official. Today, EchoHawk is a professor of law at Brigham Young University's Law School in Utah.

Judicial Branch

The judicial branch interprets the state's laws. The highest court is the state supreme court. One chief justice and four associate justices serve six-year terms. They are elected by voters. In most states, supreme court justices are appointed by the governor.

The court of appeals is the next highest court. Three judges are elected to six-year terms. Idaho has seven judicial districts. Each district has one judge elected to a four-year term.

Idaho grows more potatoes than any other state.

Chapter 5

Economy and Resources

Many Idaho license plates say "Famous Potatoes." Idaho potatoes are known around the world.

In the late 1800s, Luther Burbank experimented with potatoes in his garden in New England. He found a way to grow larger potatoes. Burbank took some of these potatoes to California. Another man, Lon Sweet, used a type of Burbank's potato to produce a potato that was resistant to disease. That potato is the famous Idaho potato, the Russet Burbank. Russet potatoes are long and thin.

Potatoes grow well in Idaho's volcanic soil. During the growing season, the warm days and cool nights are perfect for

"We're serious but not solemn about potatoes here."
—E. Thomas Hughes, founder, Potato Museum, Washington, D.C.

growing potatoes. About 90 percent of Idaho potatoes grow in the Snake River Plain. In this region, 110,000 acres (44,500 hectares) of land are irrigated for potato crops.

Other Crops

Farmers in Idaho raise more than just potatoes. Idaho farmers also raise barley, vegetables, and sugar beets. Idaho is one of the nation's largest producers of wheat. Sheep and cattle ranching have long been important parts of the Idaho economy.

Many of Idaho's agricultural products are processed in the state. Wheat is ground into flour and made into bread and other baked goods. Sugar beets are used to make sugar. Potatoes are made into french fries. They are also dehydrated and made into instant mashed potatoes.

Tourism and Service Industries

Idaho's beautiful scenery and mountains draw millions of visitors every year. During warm weather, visitors hike, camp, rock climb, fish, and hunt. During winter, people skate, snowboard, and snowmobile. They also come to ski. Idaho's most well-known ski resort is Sun Valley. Founded in 1936, Sun Valley was the site of the first ski lift. Ice skating is also popular in Sun Valley. Many competitive skaters train there.

Sun Valley has been a popular place for skiers since 1936.

Tourists also enjoy Idaho's natural scenery. Craters of the Moon National Monument is in central Idaho. This giant lava field covers 618 square miles (1,600 square kilometers). The lava came from volcanoes that erupted about 15,000 years ago. The most recent eruption in the area was about 2,000 years ago. Visitors see different types of lava and volcanic cones. They also can walk through long, narrow caves called lava tubes. The caves are made of hardened lava.

Idaho's hot springs also draw many visitors every year. They come to soak in mineral waters, thought to ease a body's aches and pains. People can soak in hot mineral water at Lava Hot Springs, just south of Pocatello.

Money from tourism supports many businesses, including resorts, restaurants, and retail stores. One of the nation's largest grocery chains, Albertsons, started in Boise in 1939. It now has 2,492 stores in 37 states.

Volcanic cones and lava beds draw visitors to Craters of the Moon National Monument.

Margaret Cobb Ailshie

Margaret Cobb moved to Boise with her parents when she was six years old. Her father, Calvin Cobb, was a rich business owner. He and his partners bought the *Idaho Daily Statesman* newspaper in 1889. Through the newspaper, Cobb worked for many improvements in the city, including telegraph lines and the arrival of the Union Pacific Railroad. Cobb died in 1928. Margaret, his only surviving child, took over the paper.

Margaret expanded the *Statesman*'s circulation. She bought the rival *Capital News* and papers published in smaller towns. She moved the paper out of its old building and into specially built headquarters. She was honest, intelligent, and energetic. Many people respected her.

Besides improving the paper, Margaret also improved Boise. She gave money to charities, arts organizations, and civic causes. When she died in 1959, she left behind a trust that continues to support local charities and the Red Cross.

Mining and Manufacturing

Mining has a long history in Idaho. Mines are less productive now than they were during the 1800s. They still produce silver, lead, zinc, gold, and phosphate, a rock that is used in fertilizer.

Manufacturing is also important to the Idaho economy. One of the world's largest wood-product companies, Boise Cascade, is based in Boise. Boise Cascade produces lumber for building and paper products.

Many other products are made in the state. Idahoans produce sheet metal, rubber, plastic, electrical equipment, and machinery. They also build prefabricated houses. In a prefabricated house, most of the construction work is done in a factory. The large pieces of the house are then trucked to the site and put together.

Fishing in Idaho's rivers is a popular sport.

Chapter 6

People and Culture

Idaho's most well-known food is the potato. The Russet Burbank is a unique potato. If you place a Russet Burbank in salty water, it will sink. Other potatoes will float. It sinks because it has a different balance of sugars and starches.

Idaho is famous not only for potatoes, but also for fish. The state is the nation's leading source of trout. Seventy-five percent of the trout eaten in the United States comes from Idaho. Salmon is another notable export of Idaho and one of the residents' favorite foods.

Idaho's People

Most of Idaho's population is white. Some of these people can trace their ancestry to Idaho's early settlers who arrived in the 1800s. Idahoans came from different European groups. English, Swedish, German, and Danish ancestry is common.

American Indians have always been an important part of Idaho. They include members of the Nez Perce, Kootenai, Coeur d'Alene, Shoshone-Bannock, and the Shoshone-Paiute tribes.

American Indians celebrate their heritage with powwows and festivals.

Idaho's Ethnic Backgrounds

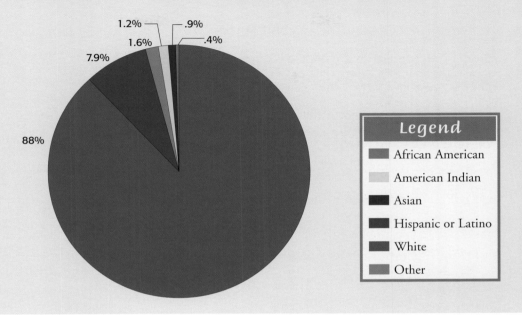

Legend
- African American
- American Indian
- Asian
- Hispanic or Latino
- White
- Other

Many other Idahoans are of Mexican ancestry. The Hispanic community is the fastest growing part of Idaho's population. It increased 92 percent from 1990 to 2000.

African Americans were the second fastest growing group during this time. In 1990, only 3,370 African Americans made their homes in the state. In 2000, that figure increased by almost 62 percent to 5,456. Visitors to Boise can learn more about Idaho's African American history at the Idaho Black History Museum.

Idaho Potatoes

To store an Idaho potato, never put it in the refrigerator. Store it in a cool, dark place. If the room is too cold, part of the potato's starch will turn into sugar. If stored in the light, the potato will turn green and bitter.

Idaho potatoes are sold for baking, mashing, and boiling. They can be made into hashbrowns, french fries, and potato salad. They can even be turned into potato flour and potato candy.

More than 11,800 Asian Americans live in Idaho. In the 1870s, most Idaho miners were Chinese. Japanese workers helped build the railroad through Idaho during the 1890s.

Boise has the country's largest group of people of Basque ancestry. The Basque are a native people of the Pyrenees Mountains, located between France and Spain. Many of them arrived between 1900 and 1920 to herd sheep on Idaho's large sheep ranges.

Bordering States

Because the land of Idaho varies so much, many Idahoans identify themselves closely with the states that border Idaho rather than with their home state. Those who live in the southeastern part of the state share the Mormon background of Utah. In the northern part, people feel more a part of Washington than Idaho. This area is part of the Inland Empire, which is centered in Spokane, Washington. The business and agricultural areas around Boise spread into Oregon.

Idaho is now more than 100 years old. It has changed a great deal from the time of Lewis and Clark. Idahoans continue to preserve the past and make use of their many natural resources.

People of Basque ancestry celebrate their heritage with dances.

Recipe: Potato Candy

The Idaho potato can be made into many foods and snacks. It can even be made into candy.

Ingredients

2 cups (480 mL) Idaho
  mashed potatoes
2 cups (480 mL) powdered
  sugar
7 ounces (195 grams)
  coconut
12 ounces (330 grams)
  chocolate chips

Equipment

medium bowl
baking pan, 9 inches by
  9 inches (23 centimeters
  by 23 centimeters)
wooden spoon
microwave-safe dish

What You Do

1. In a medium bowl, combine mashed potatoes, powdered sugar, and coconut.

2. Spread the mixture into the baking pan using the wooden spoon. Put the pan into the refrigerator for 1 hour to chill and set the candy.

3. Have an adult help you melt the chocolate chips. Put the chocolate chips into a microwave-safe dish. Heat at 50 percent power for 30 seconds. Stir. Heat for another 30 seconds and stir.

4. While the chocolate is still warm, spread it over the top of the potato mixture.

5. Put the pan into the refrigerator for another hour to harden the chocolate.

6. Cut the potato candy into squares.

Makes 16 squares

Idaho's Flag and Seal

Idaho's Flag

Idaho's state flag features the state seal in the center of a blue background. The seal shows the major industries of Idaho. The miner on the right reflects that mining was once the leading industry in Idaho. The woman on the left represents equality and justice.

Idaho's State Seal

Idaho's state seal is the only state seal designed by a woman. Emma Edwards entered her design for the state seal in a contest. She won $100 for her design. The seal has images that reflect the natural beauty of the state. A mountain stream and a white pine are featured on a shield in the center of the seal. The elk's head above the shield shows Idaho's concern for wildlife. The seal was officially adopted in 1891.

Almanac

General Facts

Nickname: Gem State

Population: 1,293,953
(U.S. Census, 2000)
Population rank: 39th

Capital: Boise

Largest cities: Boise,
Nampa, Pocatello, Idaho
Falls, Coeur d'Alene

Agriculture

Agricultural products:
Potatoes, wheat,
sugar beets, cattle,
sheep, dairy

Geography

Area: 83,574 square miles
(216,457 square kilometers)
Size rank: 14th

Highest point: Borah Peak,
12,662 feet (3,859 meters)
above sea level

Lowest point: Snake River
at Lewiston, 770 feet
(235 meters) above sea level

Climate

Average summer
temperature:
63 degrees Fahrenheit
(17 degrees Celsius)

Average winter
temperature:
25 degrees Fahrenheit
(minus 4 degrees Celsius)

Average annual
precipitation: 18.8 inches
(47.8 centimeters)

Appaloosa horse

Mountain bluebird

Bird: Mountain bluebird

Fish: Cutthroat trout

Flower: Syringa

Gemstone: Star garnet

Horse: Appaloosa

Natural resources: Silver, lead, gold, phosphate, zinc, hydroelectric power

Types of industry: Food products, wood products, computer microchips

Song: "Here We Have Idaho," words by McKinley Helm and Albert J. Tompkins; music by Sallie Hume-Douglas

Tree: Western white pine

Vegetable: Potato

First governor: George L. Shoup

Statehood: July 3, 1890 (43rd state)

U.S. Representatives: 2

U.S. Senators: 2

U.S. electoral votes: 4

Counties: 44

Timeline

State History

1805
Lewis and Clark explore Idaho.

1877
The Nez Perce surrender after three months of resistance.

1863
U.S. Congress establishes Idaho Territory, with Lewiston as the capital.

1860
Elias Pierce discovers gold at Orofino Creek.

U.S. History

1620
Pilgrims establish a colony in the New World.

1775–1783
American colonists and Great Britain fight the Revolutionary War.

1803
The United States buys the Louisiana Territory from France; the Louisiana Purchase includes what is now Idaho.

1861–1865
The Union and the Confederacy fight the Civil War.

1936
Ski resort in
Sun Valley
opens.

1951
The first electricity from
nuclear power is produced at
the National Reactor Testing
Station near Idaho Falls.

1890
On July 3,
Idaho becomes
the 43rd state.

1990
Idaho celebrates
100 years of
statehood.

1976
The Teton
Dam bursts.

1929–1939
Many Americans
lose jobs during
the Great
Depression.

1964
U.S. Congress
passes the Civil
Right Act, which
makes any form
of discrimination
illegal.

1914–1918
World War I is
fought; the
United States
enters the war
in 1917.

1939–1945
World War II is
fought; the United
States enters the
war in 1941.

2001
On September 11,
terrorists attack the
World Trade Center
and the Pentagon.

Words to Know

artificial (ar-ti-FISH-uhl)—not natural; artificial lakes are created by water pooling up behind a dam.

Basque (BASK)—a person whose ancestors are from the Pyrenees Mountains, located between France and Spain

gem (JEM)—a precious stone, such as a diamond, a ruby, or an emerald

hydroelectric power (hye-droh-e-LEK-trik POU-ur)—energy that is produced by flowing water; hydroelectric power plants are often built at dams.

internment camp (in-TURN-muhnt KAMP)—one of several places where Japanese Americans were forced to live during World War II

missionary (MISH-uh-nair-ee)—someone who is sent by a church to teach that church's beliefs

reservoir (REZ-ur-vwar)—a holding area for large amounts of water; bodies of water behind dams are often called reservoirs.

supermajority (SOO-pur-muh-JOR-uh-tee)—an overwhelming majority; Republicans greatly outnumber Democrats in the Idaho legislature, making a supermajority.

white water (WITE WAW-tur)—rough, fast-moving water in a river or stream

To Learn More

Bursell, Susan. *The Lewis and Clark Expedition.* Let Freedom Ring: Exploring the West. Mankato, Minn.: Bridgestone Books, 2002.

Foran, Jill. *Idaho.* A Kid's Guide to American States. Mankato, Minn.: Weigl, 2001.

George, Charles, and Linda George. *Idaho.* America the Beautiful. New York: Children's Press, 2000.

Patent, Dorothy Hinshaw. *Animals on the Trail with Lewis and Clark.* New York: Clarion Books, 2002.

Wallner, Rosemary. *Sacagawea, 1788–1812.* American Indian Biographies. Mankato, Minn.: Blue Earth Books, 2003.

Internet Sites

Track down many sites about Idaho.
Visit the FACT HOUND at *http://www.facthound.com*

IT IS EASY! IT IS FUN!
1) Go to *http://www.facthound.com*
2) Type in: 0736815805
3) Click on "FETCH IT" and FACT HOUND will find several links hand-picked by our editors.

Relax and let our pal FACT HOUND do the research for you!

Places to Write and Visit

Craters of the Moon National Monument
National Park Service
Park Headquarters
P.O. Box 29
Arco, ID 83213

Idaho Black History Museum
Julia Davis Park
508 North Julia Davis Drive
Boise, ID 83702

Idaho Department of Commerce
700 West State Street
Boise, ID 83720

Idaho Potato Expo
P.O. Box 366
Blackfoot, ID 83221

Office of the Governor
700 West Jefferson, 2nd Floor
P.O. Box 83720
Boise, ID 83720-0034

Coeur d'Alene Resort
sits on the shore of
Lake Coeur d'Alene.

Index

T 57075